Irrecoverable and doubtful debts

Workbook

Teresa Clarke FMAAT

Irrecoverable debts and allowance for doubtful debts workbook

By Teresa Clarke FMAAT

Chapter 1: Introduction

Many businesses sell their goods or services to their customers on credit. This means that they do not get payment immediately, but usually offer credit terms, such as 30 days net. This means that the customer has 30 days to pay the invoice.

However, some customers do not pay their invoices for a variety of reasons: They may be having financial difficulties, they may have cashflow problems, they may be unhappy with the goods supplied, etc.

An irrecoverable debt is an amount owing to the business which the business considers will not be paid. This is also referred to as a bad debt. An irrecoverable debt is usually just one invoice or the outstanding debt of one particular customer.

A doubtful debt is the amount a business estimates is unlikely to be received. The business is unsure about whether the amount will be received or not, so provision is made for this as a doubtful debt. A doubtful debt can be calculated as a percentage of all the outstanding invoices of the business, known as a general provision for doubtful debt. Or it can be a specific doubtful debt for one invoice or one particular customer's outstanding balance.

We will work through some examples of each to help you to distinguish between irrecoverable and doubtful debts.

Note:

Irrecoverable debt is also described as **bad debt**.

Allowance for doubtful debt is also described as **provision for doubtful debt**.

We will also look at how the accounting entries are made for the allowance for doubtful debt and how the accounting entries are made for the irrecoverable debts, including entries for adjustments to the VAT control account.

I will show some examples of tasks, explaining them as we work through them. Then you can have a go at some tasks on your own. Please check your answers as you go and take time to see where you have made any errors before moving on.

Remember:

Use DEAD CLIC or similar when working out your journal entries. I will refer to this throughout the workbook.

Debits increase

Expenses

Assets

Drawings

Credits increase

Liabilities

Income

Capital

Chapter 2: Examples

Example 1:

Koochet's Pet Supplies sent out goods to Sunny Kennels on 1 March 2020 at a cost of £240 including VAT. The invoice was issued the same day offering 30-day credit terms. £288
48 VAT

This means that Sunny Kennels was given 30 days from the invoice date to pay.

Due to the Covid lockdown, Sunny Kennels closed shortly after receipt of the goods and were unable to trade for many months. This meant they were unable to settle their outstanding debt with Koochet's Pet Supplies. Soon after, Sunny Kennels announced that they were closing permanently.

Koochet's Pet Supplies decided to right off this debt as irrecoverable in their accounts, as the amount outstanding was not going to be received.

Write up the journal entries required for this adjustment.

Now let's look at the journal entries for this transaction.

On 1 March 2020, the sale was entered into the accounting records.

Note that I have used the account name of Sales Ledger Control Account or SLCA, but this means the same as Trade Receivables.

Sales

Debit	£	Credit	£
		SLCA	200.00

VAT Control Account

Debit	£	Credit	£
		SLCA	40.00

Sales Ledger Control Account

Debit	£	Credit	£
Sales	200.00		
VAT	40.00		

Cr   Sales   £200.00

Cr   VAT   £ 40.00

Dr   SLCA   £240.00

Explanation:

The total sale was £240 including VAT.

Sales account was credited with £200.00, the net amount before VAT.

This was calculated like this:

£240 = 120%

£240 divided by 120 = ££2

£2 = 1%

£2 x 100 = 100%

This is the sale value before VAT.

This is a credit as it is income.

VAT was credited with £40.00.

This was calculated like this:

£240 = 120%

£240 divided by 120 = ££2

£2 = 1%

£2 x 20 = £40

£40 is the VAT amount

This is a credit because it is owed to HMRC, so a liability.

SLCA was debited with the full amount of £240 because this is the amount that the customer owes the business.

This is a debit because it is an asset to the business, money owed to the business.

The business decided to write off this debt as an irrecoverable debt, so we need to make entries to remove this from the accounting records.

We need to record this as an irrecoverable debt. Irrecoverable debts cost the business money, so they are a form of expense.

We need to record the debt as an irrecoverable debt, adjust the VAT control account and remove the amount owed from the sales ledger control account.

Irrecoverable debt expense

Debit	£	Credit	£
SLCA	200.00		

VAT control account

Debit	£	Credit	£
SLCA	40.00	SLCA	40.00

Sales ledger control account

Debit	£	Credit	£
Sales	200.00	**Irrecoverable debts**	**200.00**
VAT	40.00	**VAT control account**	**40.00**

Explanation:

The irrecoverable debt expense account is debited with £200.00 as this is the net amount that the business will not receive from the customer.
It is a debit because it is an expense to the business.

The VAT control account is debited with £40.00 as this amount is no longer owed to HMRC.
This is a debit because it reduces the liability to HMRC.

The sales ledger control account is credited with £240.00 as this whole amount is no longer a debt to the business.
This is a credit because it is reducing the asset, the amount owed to the business.

In an exam question, you are unlikely to see the first steps, the original entry into the accounting records, but take time to think about where the original entries went, and this will help you to make the adjustments. We can look at a question now which does not show those original entries.

Example 2:   DCC

Shimmering Shanaz Products has received information about one of its customers, Rusty Bolts Ltd. They have been informed that Rusty Bolts Ltd has gone out of business.

Shimmering Shanaz Products is owed £96.00, including VAT, by Rusty Bolts Ltd for an invoice sent over 2 months ago. This will not be paid now.

80 +16

You are required to make the journal entries to account for this irrecoverable debt.

Take time to think about what the original transaction was.

The total invoice was £96 including VAT, so break this down into the net amount and the VAT first.

£96 is 120%, so 96 divided by 120 = 0.80 (1%)

0.80 x 100 = £80.00 (the net amount of the sale)

0.80 x 20 = £16.00 (the VAT on the sale)

This would have been entered as:

Dr	SLCA	£96.00 (the full amount owed to the business)
Cr	Sales	£80.00 (the net sale)
Cr	VAT	£16.00 (the VAT on the sale)

If you take time to write this down first, it will help you with the adjustments for the irrecoverable debt.

Draw the t accounts for your workings, even if the answer does not require them, as it helps to see what you are doing.

Irrecoverable debt expense

Debit	£	Credit	£
SLCA	**80.00**		

VAT control account

Debit	£	Credit	£
SLCA	**16.00**		

Sales ledger control account

Debit	£	Credit	£
		Irrecoverable debts	**80.00**
		VAT control account	**16.00**

Answer:

Dr	Irrecoverable debts	£80.00
Dr	VAT	£16.00
Cr	SLCA	£96.00

Explanation:

Irrecoverable debts are an expense to the business, so this account is debited with £80.00. This increases the expenses of the business.

VAT is debited with £16.00 as this amount is no longer owed to HMRC, so reduces the liability.

The SLCA is credited with £96.00, the full amount of the invoice, as this is no longer owed to the business. It reduces the asset or money owed to the business.

Example 3:

Baiba's Beauty Products sells goods to shops, salons and other businesses across the UK. Every year she includes a general provision for doubtful debts against the total trade receivables at the end of the year. This year she has decided to put in a provision of 2% of the outstanding year end trade receivables balance as a doubtful debt.

You are required to write up the journal entries required for this adjustment.

Remember that the term 'year end trade receivables' means the balance owed to the business at the end of the year. This is the balance in the sales ledger control account at the end of the year. This is the figure we need to use to calculate the new allowance for doubtful debt.

We need to gather the information required to answer this question, so firstly we look at the existing ledgers for the sales ledger control account and the allowance for doubtful debt.

Sales ledger control account

Debit	£	Credit	£
Balance b/d	66,500		

Allowance for doubtful debt

Debit	£	Credit	£
		Balance b/d	900

We can see that both accounts have balances in them.

First, we need to calculate what the allowance for doubtful debt needs to be this year.

The question tells us that this is calculated at 2% of the outstanding trade receivables, so 2% of the SLCA balance.

£66,500 x 2% = £1,330

This is the amount that Baiba wants the allowance for doubtful debts balance to be, but we can see that there is already a balance in that account of £900.

We need to work out how can we adjust the allowance for doubtful debt so that the balance is £1,330.

£900 + something = £1,330

So that means we need to add £430 to the account to make it what we want.

£900 + £430 = £1,330.

Now let's put that adjustment into the t account and balance it off.

Allowance for doubtful debt

Debit	£	Credit	£
Balance c/d	1330	Balance b/d	900
		Allowance for doubtful debt adjustment	430
	1330		1330

But we must remember that every credit entry has a debit entry.

The adjustment of £430 that we credited to this account needs to go into the allowance for doubtful debt adjustment account.

Allowance for doubtful debt adjustment

Debit	£	Credit	£
Allowance for doubtful debt	430	**Transfer to statement of profit or loss**	430
	430		430

These are always the two accounts we use to record the allowance for doubtful debt adjustments.

Answer:

Dr   Allowance for doubtful debt adjustment   £430

Cr   Allowance for doubtful debt   £430

Example 4:

Naomi has provided you with the following extract from the trial balance.

	Dr £	Cr £
Sales ledger control account	14,500	
Purchase ledger control account		6,200
Allowance for doubtful debts		150
Irrecoverable debts	200	

Naomi would like to make provision for a specific doubtful debt of £800 and make a general provision of 1% on the remaining receivables.

You are required to make journal entries for these adjustments.

Note:

Sometimes a question will give you information you do not need, so if you don't think it is relevant, ignore it!

First, we work out what we want the doubtful debt balance to be.
Naomi wants to make provision for a specific doubtful debt of £800, so we know that has to be included.
Then she wants the provision to be 1% of the remaining receivables.

The key word here is remaining.

We take the balance on the sales ledger control account of £14,500 and deduct the £800 of specific debt, before working out the 1% of the remaining receivables.

£14,500 - £800 = £13,700

£13,700 x 1% = £137

So, the total provision for the doubtful debt is:

Specific allowance   =   £800

General allowance   =   £137

Total for doubtful debts   =   £937

This is the total that we want to adjust the allowance for doubtful debts to.

Now we can look at the allowance for doubtful debts balance. We can see from the trial balance that it already has a credit balance of £150, so we need to adjust this to £937.

£150 + ? = £937

£150 + £787 = £937

£787 is the amount we need to adjust it by.

Remember that we need to adjust the allowance for doubtful debts account and the allowance for doubtful debts adjustment account.

Allowance for doubtful debt

Debit	£	Credit	£
Balance c/d	937	Balance b/d	150
		Allowance for doubtful debt adjustment	787
	937		937

Allowance for doubtful debt adjustment

Debit	£	Credit	£
Allowance for doubtful debt	787	Transfer to SOPL	787
	787		787

Answer:

Dr   Allowance for doubtful debt adjustment   £787

Cr   Allowance for doubtful debt   £787

Note:

The allowance for doubtful debt is carried forward into the next account year, so this is entered into the statement of financial position as an allowance against the SLCA balance.

The allowance for doubtful debt adjustment is transferred to the statement of profit or loss as an increase in expenses for this year.

Example 5:

Hadi has provided you with the following information about his business at the year-end.

Balance outstanding from customers	£74,000
Bank balance	£32,000
Balance owed to suppliers	£13,500
Allowance for doubtful debt balance brought down	£1,240

Hadi wishes you to account for an irrecoverable debt of £300.

He wishes you to adjust his allowance for doubtful debts to 2% of the remaining receivables.

Make journal entries to account for these year-end adjustments.

Handwritten working:
£74,000
− 300
= 73,700
− 1474

Note:

Again, note that word remaining!

We always make entries for the irrecoverable debt first. Irrecoverable debts are an expense to the business, so these are a debit. The sales ledger control account will be reduced by this amount as this money is no longer owed to the business.

It is always good practice to draw the T accounts.

Irrecoverable debts

Debit	£	Credit	£
SLCA	300	Transfer to SOPL	300
	300		300

Sales ledger control account

Debit	£	Credit	£
Balance b/d	74,000	Irrecoverable debts	300
		Balance c/d	73,700
	74,000		74,000

Answer:

Dr   Irrecoverable debts   £300

Cr   SLCA   £300

Explanation:

I have debited the irrecoverable debts account with £300 as this is an expense to the business. This expense it then transferred to the SOPL (statement of profit or loss).

I have credited the sales ledger control account with £300 as this amount is no longer owed to the business. I have balanced the account off, and this gives us a balance c/d of £73,700, the <u>remaining</u> balance on the SLCA.

Hadi wishes to adjust the allowance for doubtful debts account to 2% of the remaining receivables, so we can use the <u>remaining</u> balance of £73,700 to calculate the amount we want the allowance for doubtful debts to be.

£73,700 x 2% = £1,474

This is the balance we want the allowance for doubtful debts to be.

We can see from the information provided that the allowance for doubtful debts already has a balance of £1,240, so we start by drawing up the t accounts.

Allowance for doubtful debt

Debit	£	Credit	£
Balance c/d	1,474	Balance b/d	1,240
		Allowance for doubtful debt adjustment	234
	1,474		1,474

Allowance for doubtful debt adjustment

Debit	£	Credit	£
Allowance for doubtful debt	234	Transfer to SOPL	234
	234		234

Answer:

Cr   Allowance for doubtful debt   £234

Dr   Allowance for doubtful debt adjustment   £234

Note:

Although it is strictly correct to put debit entries first, you are not penalised for this in level 2 or 3 exams.

Explanation:

The allowance for doubtful debt already had a balance of £1,240, so I credited it with a further £234 to make the figure of £1,474 that we wanted. This would be carried down into the next financial period, so entered in the statement of financial position.

The allowance for doubtful debt adjustment was debited with £234 increasing the expense. This is transferred to the statement of profit or loss.

Example 6:

Janice has provided you with the following information:

The balance on the sales ledger control account at the end of the year is £12,500 and the balance on the allowance for doubtful debts account brought down from last year is £500.

Janice would like to adjust the allowance for doubtful debts account to 3% of the outstanding receivables.

You are required to make the required journal entries to account for this.

We start by calculating the required doubtful debt figure at the year-end. The SLCA balance is £12,500 and we want to the allowance for doubtful debt to be 3% of that.

£12,500 x 3% = £375

Now we draw up the T accounts, making sure that we put in the balance on the allowance for doubtful debts account. Then enter the required adjustment.

Allowance for doubtful debt

Debit	£	Credit	£
Allowance for doubtful debt adjustment	125	Balance b/d	500
Balance c/d	375		
	500		500

Allowance for doubtful debt adjustment

Debit	£	Credit	£
Transfer to SOPL	125	**Allowance for doubtful debt**	125
	125		125

Answer:

Dr   Allowance for doubtful debts   £125

Cr   Allowance for doubtful debts adjustment   £125

Explanation:

This task was slightly different because we needed to reduce the balance in the allowance for doubtful debts account, rather than increase it. This meant that we needed to debit it with £125 to lower the balance to carry down to £375. The allowance for doubtful debt adjustment account was therefore credited with £125 reducing the expense in that year.

This is one to watch, as the adjustment account can be entered on either side, depending on whether we are increasing or decreasing the balance on the allowance for doubtful debt.

Some points to remember:

An irrecoverable debt is money owed to the business which it believes will never be paid.

Irrecoverable debt = bad debt.

An allowance for doubtful debt is a provision for money owed to the business which it believes are unlikely to be paid.

Allowance for doubtful debt = provision for doubtful debt

Irrecoverable debt journal entries:

Dr Irrecoverable debts
Cr Sales ledger control account

Sales ledger control account = trade receivables

Allowance for doubtful debt journal entries for an increase

Dr Allowance for doubtful debts adjustment
Cr Allowance for doubtful debts

Allowance for doubtful debt journal entries for a decrease

Dr Allowance for doubtful debts
Cr Allowance for doubtful debts adjustment

Chapter 3: Tasks

Answers and workings in Chapter 4, page 52

Task 1:

Ulita and Gill are in partnership letting out holiday cottages in Norfolk. Their supplies are all exempt from VAT, so you can ignore VAT in this question. The trade receivables or SLCA balance at the end of the year was £11,200.

At the end of the financial year, Ulita and Gill have asked you to complete the following adjustments to the accounting records.

A) Write off an irrecoverable debt of £200.
B) Make a doubtful debt provision of 1% of the <u>remaining</u> receivables at the year-end.

Complete the following journals for these adjustments.
Use the T accounts for your workings.

A

Journal	Dr	Cr

B

Journal	Dr	Cr

Debit	£	Credit	£

Debit	£	Credit	£

Debit	£	Credit	£

Debit	£	Credit	£

Task 2:

Charlie's trial balance shows trade receivables with a balance of £46,000 and an allowance for doubtful debt of £2,500.

Charlie wishes to adjust the allowance for doubtful debt to 5% of the receivables.

What will be the accounting entries to make this adjustment?

Journal	Dr	Cr

Use the T accounts below for your workings.

Debit	£	Credit	£

Debit	£	Credit	£

Debit	£	Credit	£

Task 3:

Janice has provided you with the following information from her trial balance.

	Dr £	Cr £
Trade receivables balance	16,400	
Allowance for doubtful debts		610

She needs to write off an irrecoverable debt of £200, allow for a specific doubtful debt of £400 and make a general allowance for doubtful debt of 2% of the remaining receivables.

You are required to make the journal entries for these adjustments.

Journal	Dr	Cr

Journal	Dr	Cr

Hint:

Irrecoverable debts first, then the maths for the doubtful debts. Don't forget to draw the T accounts. Blank ones are shown below for your workings.

Debit	£	Credit	£

Debit	£	Credit	£

Debit	£	Credit	£

Debit	£	Credit	£

Task 4:

a) Janice's statement of profit or loss for the year shows a profit of £28,900.

Janice wishes to decrease the allowance for doubtful debt by £400.

Calculate the adjusted profit for the year.

b) Tammer's statement of profit or loss for the year shows a loss of £5,400.

Tammer wishes to increase the allowance for doubtful debt by £500.

Calculate the adjusted loss for the year.

Here are some T accounts for your workings:

Debit	£	Credit	£

Debit	£	Credit	£

Debit	£	Credit	£

Debit	£	Credit	£

Task 5:

a) Alicja's statement of profit or loss for the year shows a profit of £32,000.

She wishes to adjust this for an irrecoverable debt of £350.

What affect will this have on her profit for the year?

Tick ONE correct answer.

Her profit will increase by £350.	
There will be no change to her profit.	
Her adjusted profit will be £32,350.	
Her profit will decrease by £350.	

b) Tofan's statement of profit or loss for the year shows a loss of £3,600.

He has asked you to make adjustments for a decrease of £200 to the allowance for doubtful debt.

What affect will this have on his loss for the year?

Tick ONE correct answer.

His loss will decrease by £200.	
His adjusted loss will be £3,800.	
There will be no change in the loss for the year.	
His loss will increase by £200.	

Task 6:

Charlotte has provided you with the following extract from her trial balance.

	Dr £	Cr £
Sales revenue		130,000
Sales ledger control account	11,200	
Allowance for doubtful debt		900
Allowance for doubtful debt adjustment		
Purchase ledger control account		6,200
Irrecoverable debt		

She has decided to write off irrecoverable debts of £400 and adjust her allowance for doubtful debt to 2% of the remaining receivables.

You are required to make necessary entries into the adjustment columns below.

Use this space for your workings and there are T accounts below too.

Debit	£	Credit	£

Debit	£	Credit	£

Debit	£	Credit	£

Debit	£	Credit	£

Irrecoverable and doubtful debts workbook

	Dr £	Cr £	Adjustments Dr £	Adjustments Cr £
Sales revenue		130,000		
Sales ledger control account	11,200			
Allowance for doubtful debt		900		
Allowance for doubtful debt adjustment				
Purchase ledger control account		6,200		
Irrecoverable debt				

Remember to make your adjustments in the adjustment columns only.

Task 7:

Complete the following sentences.

a) The allowance for doubtful debt account is entered into the **statement of financial position / statement of profit or loss**.

b) An increase in the allowance for doubtful debt will be entered as a **debit / credit** in the allowance for doubtful debt account.

c) A decrease in the allowance for doubtful debt will **increase / decrease** the profit for the year.

d) An irrecoverable debt will **increase / decrease** profit for the year.

e) An irrecoverable debt will be entered as an **expense / income** in the statement of profit or loss.

f) A debit entry in the allowance for doubtful debts adjustment account will be shown as an **expense / other income** in the **statement of financial position / statement of profit or loss**.

Task 8:

Tatiana has been preparing the financial statements for Pardeep's Plant Hire for the year ended 31 March 2022.

She has discovered that an irrecoverable debt of £800 should have been written off.

Prior to making any adjustments the balances in the sales ledger control account and allowance for doubtful debt accounts were:

| Sales ledger control account | £14,000 |
| Allowance for doubtful debts | £480 |

The allowance for doubtful debts account will need to be adjusted to 4% of the remaining receivables at the year-end.

You are required to make journal entries for the irrecoverable debt and the allowance for doubtful debt.

Use the T accounts for your workings.

Debit	£	Credit	£

Debit	£	Credit	£

Debit	£	Credit	£

Debit	£	Credit	£

Debit	£	Credit	£

Journal	Dr	Cr

Journal	Dr	Cr

Task 9:

Karen and Kate have provided the following information from their accounting records for the year ended 31 March 2022.

Ledger balances

Sales ledger control account	£7,500
Purchase ledger control account	£3,200
Allowance for doubtful debts	£400

They wish to adjust the accounting records to take into account the following:

An irrecoverable debt of £150.

A specific allowance for doubtful debt on an invoice to Carly's Stores for £200 which they believe will not be paid.

A general allowance on the remaining receivables of 5%.

You are required to make the necessary journal entries for these adjustments.

Round your answers to the nearest whole pound.

Use the workings box and T accounts for your calculations and workings.

Irrecoverable and doubtful debts workbook

Workings

Debit	£	Credit	£

Debit	£	Credit	£

Debit	£	Credit	£

Debit	£	Credit	£

Answers:

Journal	Dr	Cr

Journal	Dr	Cr

Task 10:

a) Tracy has a balance brought down of £320 on her allowance for doubtful debt account.

She has a balance on her sales ledger control account of £4,500.

She has a policy of adjusting the allowance for doubtful debts to 5% of the receivables balance.

What is the value of the adjustment that she needs to make to her allowance for doubtful debts account?

Pick ONE correct answer.

£225	
£545	
£95	
£415	

b) Referring to your answer above, will this entry be a debit or credit in the allowance for doubtful debts account?

Debit	
Credit	

Task 11:

Read through the following and identify whether the statements are true or false.

	True	False
Irrecoverable debts are also known as bad debts.		
The balance on the allowance for doubtful debts account will always be on the credit side.		
Irrecoverable debts are an expense to the business.		
Allowance for doubtful debt is also known as provision for doubtful debt.		
A decrease in the allowance for doubtful debt will be a debit in the allowance for doubtful debt adjustment account.		
An increase in the allowance for doubtful debts will increase the profit for the business.		
An increase in the allowance for doubtful debts will mean an expense in the statement of profit or loss.		
An irrecoverable debt is money that the business is not expecting to be paid.		
An allowance for doubtful debt is deducted from the sales ledger control balance in the statement of financial position.		

Task 12:

Mafalda, Norin and Niki are in partnership, running a business supplying consumables to the restaurant industry.

You have been provided with the following information at the year-end.

The trade receivables balance at the year-end is £32,500. The balance on the allowance for doubtful debts account is £1,200.

The partners have decided that they would like to make allowance for the following.

Bad debts of £326.

Specific allowance for doubtful debt of £574.

A general allowance against remaining receivables of 3%.

a) Make journal entries for the bad debt.

Journal	Dr	Cr

Blank T accounts are shown on the next page.

Debit	£	Credit	£

Debit	£	Credit	£

b) Make journal entries for the allowance for doubtful debt.

Journal	Dr	Cr

c) Complete the allowance for doubtful debts account, clearly showing the balance brought down.

Debit	£	Credit	£

d) Enter the new balances in the extract of the trial balance below.

	Dr	Cr
Sales ledger control account		
Allowance for doubtful debt		
Allowance for doubtful debt adjustment		
Irrecoverable debts		

Chapter 4: Answers

Task 1:

Ulita and Gill are in partnership letting out holiday cottages in Norfolk. Their supplies are all exempt from VAT, so you can ignore VAT in this question. The trade receivables or SLCA balance at the end of the year was £11,200.

At the end of the financial year, Ulita and Gill have asked you to complete the following adjustments to the accounting records.

A) Write off an irrecoverable debt of £200.
B) Make a doubtful debt provision of 1% of the <u>remaining</u> receivables at the year-end.

Complete the following journals for these adjustments.

A

Journal	Dr £	Cr £
Irrecoverable debts	200	
SLCA / trade receivables		200

B

Journal	Dr £	Cr £
Allowance for doubtful debt		110
Allowance for doubtful debt adjustment	110	

Workings and explanation:

A   The irrecoverable debt is an expense to the business, so this is debited. The sales ledger control balance or trade receivables balance is credited because this is being reduced because this money is no longer owed to the business.

B   The allowance for doubtful debt is calculated on the <u>remaining</u> receivables balance.

£11,200 less the irrecoverable debt of £200 = £11,000

£11,000 x 1% = £110

This is credited to the allowance for doubtful debt account to increase the (potential) liability against the sales ledger control account. The allowance for doubtful debt adjustment account is debited with the same amount, as an expense to the business.

Hint:

To remember that the allowance for doubtful debt account is a credit, remember that this is always on the opposite side to the SLCA as it is an allowance for some of that money that may not be received.

Task 2:

Charlie's trial balance shows trade receivables with a balance of £46,000 and an allowance for doubtful debt of £2,500.

Charlie wishes to adjust the allowance for doubtful debt to 5% of the receivables.

What will be the accounting entries to make this adjustment?

Journal	Dr	Cr
Allowance for doubtful debts	200	
Allowance for doubtful debt adjustment		200

Workings and explanation:

The trade receivables balance is £46,000 and we want the allowance for doubtful debt to be 5% of this.

£46,000 x 5% = £2,300

The allowance for doubtful debts already has a balance of £2,500, so we need to reduce this by £200. (£2,500 – £200 = £2,300).

The balance of the allowance for doubtful debt is on the credit side, so we need to debit this with the £200 to make our adjustment. See T account below.

Allowance for doubtful debt

Debit	£	Credit	£
Allowance for doubtful debt adjustment	200	Balance b/d	2,500
Balance c/d	2,300		
	2,500		2,500

Allowance for doubtful debt adjustment

Debit	£	Credit	£
Transfer to SOPL	200	Allowance for doubtful debt	200
	200		200

Task 3:

Janice has provided you with the following information from her trial balance.

	Dr £	Cr £
Trade receivables balance	16,400	
Allowance for doubtful debts		610

She needs to write off an irrecoverable debt of £200, allow for a specific doubtful debt of £400 and make a general allowance for doubtful debt of 2% of the remaining receivables.

You are required to make the journal entries for these adjustments.

Journal	Dr £	Cr £
Irrecoverable debt	**200**	
Sales ledger control account		**200**

Journal	Dr £	Cr £
Allowance for doubtful debt		**106**
Allowance for doubtful debt adjustment	**106**	

Hint:

Irrecoverable debts first, then the maths for the doubtful debts. Don't forget to draw the T accounts. Blank ones are shown below for your workings.

Irrecoverable debts

Debit	£	Credit	£
SLCA	200	Transfer to SOPL	200
	200		200

Sales ledger control account

Debit	£	Credit	£
Balance b/d	16,400	Irrecoverable debts	200
		Balance c/d	16,200
	16,400		16,400

Allowance for doubtful debts

Debit	£	Credit	£
		Balance b/d	610
		Allowance for doubtful debt adjustment	106
Balance c/d	716		
	716		716

Allowance for doubtful debts adjustment

Debit	£	Credit	£
Allowance for doubtful debt	106	Transfer to SOPL	106
	106		106

Workings and explanation:

The irrecoverable debt is dealt with first. This is an expense, so the irrecoverable debts is debited with £200. This reduces the amount that the business is owed, so reduces the SLCA, so the SLCA is credited with £200.

The doubtful debt calculation is in two parts.

There is a specific allowance of £400, which needs to be included.

Then we need to calculate 2% of the remaining receivables.

SLCA balance = £16,400

The irrecoverable debt reduces this by £200

£16,400 - £200 = £16,200

The specific debt of £400 is also deducted.

£16,200 - £400 = £15,800

Then we can calculate 2% of the remaining receivables.

£15,800 x 2% = £316

We have a specific allowance for doubtful debt of £400 and a general allowance for doubtful debt of £316. We add these two together and this is what we want our allowance for doubtful debt to be adjusted to.

£400 + £316 = £716.

The balance brought down in the allowance for doubtful debt account is £610, so we need to increase this to £716.

£610 + ? = £716

£610 + £106 = £716

We need to make an adjustment of £106 to this account. We credit the allowance for doubtful debt by this amount to give us the balance of £716 that we wanted.

We debit the allowance for doubtful debt adjustment account with the same amount.

Task 4:

a) Janice's statement of profit or loss for the year shows a profit of £28,900.

Janice wishes to decrease the allowance for doubtful debt by £400.

Calculate the adjusted profit for the year.

> **The decrease in the doubtful debt will be posted as a debit in the allowance for doubtful debt account and a credit in the allowance for doubtful debt adjustment account. As it is a credit in the adjustment account this reduces the expense to the business. Therefore, the profit of £28,900 will be increased by £400.**
>
> **Answer: £29,300 profit**

Allowance for doubtful debts

Debit	£	Credit	£
Allowance for doubtful debt adjustment	400		

Allowance for doubtful debt adjustment

Debit	£	Credit	£
		Allowance for doubtful debt	400

b) Tammer's statement of profit or loss for the year shows a loss of £5,400. Tammer wishes to increase the allowance for doubtful debt by £500. Calculate the adjusted loss for the year.

The increase in the doubtful debt will be posted as a credit in the allowance for doubtful debt account and a debit in the allowance for doubtful debt adjustment account. As it is a debit in the adjustment account this increases the expense to the business. Therefore, the loss of £5,400 will be increased by £500.

Answer: £5,900 loss

Allowance for doubtful debt

Debit	£	Credit	£
		All for d/d adjustment	500

Allowance for doubtful debt adjustment

Debit	£	Credit	£
All for doubtful debt	**500**		

Task 5:

a) Alicja's statement of profit or loss for the year shows a profit of £32,000.

She wishes to adjust this for an irrecoverable debt of £350.

What affect will this have on her profit for the year?

Tick ONE correct answer.

Her profit will increase by £350.	
There will be no change to her profit.	
Her adjusted profit will be £32,350.	
Her profit will decrease by £350.	√

Explanation:

The irrecoverable debt is an expense to the business, so if her expenses are increased, then her profit decreases. She makes less money.

b) Tofan's statement of profit or loss for the year shows a loss of £3,600.

He has asked you to make adjustments for a decrease of £200 to the allowance for doubtful debt.

What affect will this have on his loss for the year?

Tick ONE correct answer.

His loss will decrease by £200.	√
His adjusted loss will be £3,800.	
There will be no change in the loss for the year.	
His loss will increase by £200.	

Explanation:

The allowance for doubtful debt is reduced, which reduces the expense to the business. If the expenses are reduced this would increase a profit. Because we started with a loss in this question, then it will reduce the loss.

Task 6:

Charlotte has provided you with the following extract from her trial balance.

	Dr	Cr
Sales revenue		130,000
Sales ledger control account	11,200	
Allowance for doubtful debt		900
Allowance for doubtful debt adjustment		
Purchase ledger control account		6,200
Irrecoverable debt		

She has decided to write off irrecoverable debts of £400 and adjust her allowance for doubtful debt to 2% of the remaining receivables.

You are required to make necessary entries into the adjustment columns below.

Workings and explanation:

The irrecoverable debt is an expense to the business, so this is a debit entry.

The SLCA is reduced by this amount as the money is no longer receivable.

This entry is a credit to reduce the balance on the SLCA or receivables.

The doubtful debt needs to be adjusted to 2% of the remaining receivables.

SLCA balance £11,200, minus the irrecoverable debt written off of £400 = £10,800.

£10,800 x 2% = £216

£216 is the allowance for doubtful debt that we want showing in the accounts.

There is already a balance in the allowance for doubtful debts of £900.

We need to reduce this to £216.

£900 - ? = £216

£900 – £684 = £216

We need to reduce the allowance for doubtful debts by £684, so we debit this account.

We credit the allowance for doubtful debts with the same amount.

Irrecoverable debts

Debit	£	Credit	£
SLCA	400	Transfer to SOPL	400
	400		400

SLCA

Debit	£	Credit	£
Bal b/d	11,200	Irrecoverable debts	400
		Bal c/d	10,800
	11,200		11,200

Allowance for doubtful debt

Debit	£	Credit	£
All for d/d adjustment	**684**	**Bal b/d**	900
Bal c/d	216		
	900		900

Allowance for doubtful debt adjustment

Debit	£	Credit	£
Transfer to SOPL	684	**All for doubtful debts**	684
	684		684

If you have used the T accounts for your workings, transfer your entries into the extract of the trial balance in exactly the same way you entered them into the T accounts.

			Adjustments	
	Dr	Cr	Dr	Cr
Sales revenue		130,000		
Sales ledger control account	11,200			400
Allowance for doubtful debt		900	684	
Allowance for doubtful debt adjustment				684
Purchase ledger control account		6,200		
Irrecoverable debt			400	

Task 7:

Complete the following sentences.

a) The allowance for doubtful debt account is entered into the **statement of financial position** / ~~statement of profit or loss~~.

b) An increase in the allowance for doubtful debt will be entered as a ~~debit~~ / **credit** in the allowance for doubtful debt account.

c) A decrease in the allowance for doubtful debt will **increase** / ~~decrease~~ the profit for the year.

d) An irrecoverable debt will ~~increase~~ / **decrease** profit for the year.

e) An irrecoverable debt will be entered as an **expense** / ~~income~~ in the statement of profit or loss.

f) A debit entry in the allowance for doubtful debts adjustment account will be shown as an **expense** / ~~other income~~ in the ~~statement of financial position~~ / **statement of profit or loss**.

Explanations:

a) The allowance for doubtful debt account is entered into the statement of financial position because it reduces the balance in the sales ledger control account, which is also in this statement.

b) An increase in the allowance for doubtful debt will be a credit in this account as it increases the balance in this account.

c) A decrease in the allowance for doubtful debt reduces the expense, so increases the profit.

d) An irrecoverable debt is an expense so this will reduce the profit.

e) An irrecoverable debt is an expense as it costs the business money.

f) A debit entry in the allowance for doubtful debt adjustment account is an expense to the business and expenses are entered into the statement of profit or loss.

Task 8:

Tatiana has been preparing the financial statements for Pardeep's Plant Hire for the year ended 31 March 2022.

She has discovered that an irrecoverable debt of £800 should have been written off.

Prior to making any adjustments the balances in the sales ledger control account and allowance for doubtful debt accounts were:

| Sales ledger control account | £14,000 |
| Allowance for doubtful debts | £480 |

The allowance for doubtful debts account will need to be adjusted to 4% of the remaining receivables at the year-end.

You are required to make journal entries for the irrecoverable debt and the allowance for doubtful debt.

Journal	Dr	Cr
Irrecoverable debts	**800**	
Sales ledger control account		**800**

Journal	Dr	Cr
Allowance for doubtful debt		**48**
Allowance for doubtful debt adjustment	**48**	

Explanation and workings:

The irrecoverable debt is dealt with first. This is a debit in the irrecoverable debts account as this is an expense and is a credit in the sales ledger control account as it reduces the amount owed to the business.

Irrecoverable debts

Debit	£	Credit	£
SLCA	800	Transfer to SOPL	800
	800		800

Sales ledger control account

Debit	£	Credit	£
Bal b/d	14,000	Irrecoverable debts	800
		Bal c/d	13,200
	14,000		14,000

The allowance for doubtful debt needs to be adjusted to 4% of the remaining balance.

SLCA balance was £14,000, less the irrecoverable debt of £800 = £13,200.

£13,200 x 4% = £528.

The allowance for doubtful debts account already has a credit balance of £480. We need to increase this to £528, so we need to credit a further £48 to the allowance for doubtful debts account.

The allowance for doubtful debts adjustment account will be debited with the £48, increasing the expense to the business.

Allowance for doubtful debts

Debit	£	Credit	£
Bal c/d	528	**Bal b/d**	480
		All for d/d adjustment	48
	528		528

Allowance for doubtful debts adjustment

Debit	£	Credit	£
All for doubtful debts	48	Transfer to SOPL	48
	48		48

Task 9:

Karen and Kate have provided the following information from their accounting records for the year ended 31 March 2022.

Ledger balances

Sales ledger control account	£7,500
Purchase ledger control account	£3,200
Allowance for doubtful debts	£400

They wish to adjust the accounting records to take into account the following:

An irrecoverable debt of £150.

A specific allowance for doubtful debt on an invoice to Carly's Stores for £200 which they believe will not be paid.

A general allowance on the remaining receivables of 5%.

You are required to make the necessary journal entries for these adjustments.

Round your answers to the nearest whole pound.

Journal	Dr	Cr
Irrecoverable debts	150	
Sales ledger control account		150

Journal	Dr	Cr
Allowance for doubtful debts		158
Allowance for doubtful debts adjustment	158	

Workings and explanation:

The irrecoverable debt is written off first by debiting the irrecoverable debts account and crediting the sales ledger control account.

Irrecoverable debts

Debit	£	Credit	£
SLCA	150	Transfer to SOPL	150
	150		150

Sales ledger control account

Debit	£	Credit	£
Bal b/d	7,500	Irrecoverable debts	150
		Balance c/d	7,350
	7,500		7,500

There is a specific allowance for doubtful debt of £200, plus a general allowance of 5% on the remaining receivables.

SLCA balance is £7,500.

First, we take off the irrecoverable debt of £150 and take off the specific allowance of £200.

£7,500 - £150 - £200 = £7,150.

£7,150 is the remaining receivables balance.

£7,150 x 5% = £357.50

The question told us to round answers to the nearest whole pound, so this is £358.

Remember if a number is less than 5 we round down, or 5 and over we round up.

The general allowance for doubtful debts required is £358 and we add to that the specific allowance of £200, giving us a total of £558 for the required allowance for doubtful debt.

The allowance for doubtful debts account already has a balance of £400 so we need to increase that by £158 by crediting this account and debiting the adjustment account.

Allowance for doubtful debts

Debit	£	Credit	£
Bal c/d	558	**Bal b/d**	400
		All for doubtful debt adj	158
	558		558

Allowance for doubtful debts adjustment

Debit	£	Credit	£
All for doubtful debts	158	**Transfer to SOPL**	158
	158		158

Task 10:

a) Tracy has a balance brought forward of £320 on her allowance for doubtful debt account.

She has a balance on her sales ledger control account of £4,500.

She has a policy of adjusting the allowance for doubtful debts to 5% of the receivables balance.

What is the value of the adjustment that she needs to make to her allowance for doubtful debts account?

Pick ONE correct answer.

£225	
£545	
£95	√
£415	

b) Referring to your answer above, will this entry be a debit or credit in the allowance for doubtful debts account?

Debit	√
Credit	

Workings and explanation:

£4,500 x 5% = £225

Balance in allowance for doubtful debts is £320, so we need to reduce this.

£320 - £95 = £225

This is a debit entry in the allowance for doubtful debts. This can be seen better by drawing a T account, which is always a good idea.

Allowance for doubtful debts

Debit	£	Credit	£
		Balance b/d	**320**
All for d/d adjustment	**95**		
Balance c/d	**225**		
	320		320
		Balance b/d	**225**

By drawing the T account, you can see the original entry, the adjustment and the balance brought down.

Task 11:

Read through the following and identify whether the statements are true or false.

	True	False
Irrecoverable debts are also known as bad debts.	√	
The balance on the allowance for doubtful debts account will always be on the credit side.	√	
Irrecoverable debts are an expense to the business.	√	
Allowance for doubtful debts is also known as provision for doubtful debt.	√	
A decrease in the allowance for doubtful debt will be a debit in the allowance for doubtful debt adjustment account.		√
An increase in the allowance for doubtful debts will increase the profit for the business.		√
An increase in the allowance for doubtful debts will mean an expense in the statement of profit or loss.	√	
An irrecoverable debt is money that the business is not expecting to be paid.	√	
An allowance for doubtful debt is deducted from the sales ledger control balance in the statement of financial position.	√	

Explanations:

Irrecoverable debts are known as bad debts, mainly because it is easier to say, and spell.

The balance on the allowance for doubtful debts account is always a credit as this reduces the SLCA balance. This is not to be confused to adjustments to this, as they can be debits or credits depending on whether the allowance is being increased or reduced.

Irrecoverable debts cost the business money, so they are an expense.

Allowance for doubtful debt if often known as provision for doubtful debt, particularly in some software packages.

A decrease in the allowance for doubtful debt will be a debit in the allowance for doubtful debt, so a credit in the adjustment account.

An increase in the allowance for doubtful debt increases the expenses, so reduces the profit.

An increase in the allowance for doubtful debt increases the expenses and this is shown in the statement of profit or loss.

An irrecoverable debt is money that this business does not expect to receive, and this could be for a number of reasons, including the customer's business has gone into liquidation, the customer has moved away, the customer refuses to pay and it is too costly to take them to Court etc.

The allowance for doubtful debt is deducted from the sales ledger control account balance in the statement of financial position to give a realistic figure for the trade receivables at the end of the financial year.

Task 12:

Mafalda, Norin and Niki are in partnership, running a business supplying consumables to the restaurant industry.

You have been provided with the following information at the year-end.

The trade receivables balance at the year-end is £32,500. The balance on the allowance for doubtful debts account is £1,200.

The partners have decided that they would like to make allowance for the following.

Bad debts of £326.

Specific allowance for doubtful debt of £574.

A general allowance against remaining receivables of 3%.

a) Make journal entries for the bad debt.

Journal	Dr	Cr
Irrecoverable debts	326	
Sales ledger control account		326

Irrecoverable and doubtful debts workbook

Irrecoverable debts

Debit	£	Credit	£
SLCA	326	Transfer to SOPL	326
	326		326

Sales ledger control account

Debit	£	Credit	£
Bal b/d	32,500	Irrecoverable debts	326
		Balance c/d	32,174
	32,500		32,500

b) Make journal entries for the allowance for doubtful debt.

Journal	Dr	Cr
Allowance for doubtful debts		322
Allowance for doubtful debt adjustment	322	

Workings:

Trade receivables balance of £32,500, less the irrecoverable debt of £326, less the specific allowance of £574 = £31,600.

£31,600 x 3% = £948.

Add the specific allowance and general allowance together.

£948 + £574 = £1,522

The balance in the allowance for doubtful debts was £1,200 so we need to add £322 to that to make it up to £1,522.

We credit the allowance for doubtful debt to increase the balance.

We debit the allowance for doubtful debt adjustment account to increase the expense.

c) Complete the allowance for doubtful debts account, clearly showing the balance brought down.

Debit	£	Credit	£
		Balance b/d	1,200
		All for d/d adjustment	322
Balance c/d	1,522		
	1,522		1,522
		Balance b/d	1,522

d) Enter the new balances in the extract of the trial balance below.

	Dr	Cr
Sales ledger control account	32,174	
Allowance for doubtful debt		1,522
Allowance for doubtful debt adjustment	322	
Irrecoverable debts	326	

Explanations:

The sales ledger control account balance is reduced by the irrecoverable debt, as per the journal entry in answer a) above.

The allowance for doubtful debts new balance is £1,522, as per the T account in c) above.

The allowance for doubtful debt adjustment account has an entry of £322 for the adjustment only, as per the answer to b) above.

The irrecoverable debts account has a debit entry of £326 as per answer a) above.

Remember, that this is only an extract of a trial balance, so the sides will not balance.

I hope you have found this workbook useful. If you have any comments, you can find me on my Facebook page, Teresa Clarke Accountancy Tutoring.

You can find links of my workbooks on my website https://www.teresaclarke.co.uk/books/

Teresa Clarke FMAAT

Printed in Great Britain
by Amazon